BE A HAMSTER AND GUINEA PIG EXPERT

Be A Pet Expert

By Gemma Barder

CRABTREE
PUBLISHING COMPANY
WWW.CRABTREEBOOKS.COM

BE A HAMSTER AND GUINEA PIG EXPERT

Hamsters and guinea pigs make great pets. They are fun, energetic, and playful, but how much do you know about these furry mini mammals? In this book you'll find advice on which pet to choose, how to make the perfect home for it, and how to keep your pet happy and healthy. Plus there are some absolutely paw-some hamster and guinea pig facts to discover. How did guinea pigs become pets? What is the world's biggest **rodent**? Keep reading to find out!

Published in Canada
Crabtree Publishing
616 Welland Avenue
St. Catharines, ON
L2M 5V6

Published in the United States
Crabtree Publishing
347 Fifth Ave,
Suite 1402-145
New York, NY 10016

Published in 2021 by CRABTREE PUBLISHING COMPANY.

First published in 2019 by Wayland
Copyright © Hodder and Stoughton, 2019

Author: Gemma Barder

Editorial director: Kathy Middleton

Editors: Dynamo Limited, Robin Johnson

Cover and interior design: Dynamo Limited

Proofreader: Melissa Boyce

**Production coordinator
& Prepress technician:** Samara Parent

Print coordinator: Katherine Berti

Printed in the U.S.A./072020/CG20200429

Photographs
(l - left, r - right, br - bottom right, bc - bottom center, cl - center left, cr - center right, tr - top right)

All images courtesy of Getty Images iStock except:
© Film Company Disney/AF Archive/Alamy: 20cl; Lynne Cameron/PA Archive/PAi: 20b; ImageBroker/Alamy: 3tr, 7tr, 29bl; Eric Isselee/Shutterstock: front cover r, title page r; Sonja Jordan/Alamy: 7c, 28br; Igor Kovalchuk/Shutterstock: front cover l, 1l; Kristo-Gothard Hunor/Shutterstock: 14cr; Bozena Fulawka: 15bc; Tierfotoagentur/Alamy: 5br; © Universal Pictures/Entertainment Pictures/Alamy: 21c; stock_shot/Shutterstock: 24t

Every attempt has been made to clear copyright. Should there be any inadvertent omission, please apply to the publisher for rectification.

Library and Archives Canada Cataloguing in Publication

Title: Be a hamster and guinea pig expert / by Gemma Barder.
Other titles: Hamsters and guinea pigs
Names: Barder, Gemma, author.
Description: Series statement: Be a pet expert | Previously published under title: Hamsters and guinea pigs. | Includes index.
Identifiers: Canadiana (print) 20200222570 |
　Canadiana (ebook) 20200222600 |
　ISBN 9780778780175 (hardcover) |
　ISBN 9780778780458 (softcover) |
　ISBN 9781427125590 (HTML)
Subjects: LCSH: Hamsters as pets—Juvenile literature. | LCSH: Guinea pigs as pets—Juvenile literature. | LCSH: Hamsters—Juvenile literature. | LCSH: Guinea pigs—Juvenile literature.
Classification: LCC SF459.H3 B37 2021 | DDC j636.935/6—dc23

Library of Congress Cataloging-in-Publication Data

Names: Barder, Gemma, author.
Title: Be a hamster and guinea pig expert / by Gemma Barder.
Description: New York : Crabtree Publishing Company, 2021. |
　Series: Be a pet expert | Includes index.
Identifiers: LCCN 2020015994 (print) | LCCN 2020015995 (ebook) |
　ISBN 9780778780175 (hardcover) |
　ISBN 9780778780458 (paperback) |
　ISBN 9781427125590 (ebook)
Subjects: LCSH: Hamsters as pets--Juvenile literature. |
　Guinea pigs as pets--Juvenile literature.
Classification: LCC SF459.H3 B335 2021 (print) | LCC SF459.H3 (ebook) |
　DDC 636.935/6--dc23
LC record available at https://lccn.loc.gov/2020015994
LC ebook record available at https://lccn.loc.gov/2020015995

CONTENTS

LITTLE PET, BIG LOVE!

SCURRY THROUGH TIME

FURRY FRIENDS

Learn all about the most popular types of hamsters and guinea pigs. The little things that make them different will help you choose the best pet for you.

AMERICAN GUINEA PIG

The American guinea pig is the most popular **breed** of guinea pig in the world. It has a calm, sweet nature and a soft, easy-to-manage **coat**, which makes it the perfect pet. It is happiest when spending time with other guinea pigs and its owner.

HAMSTERS vs. GUINEA PIGS

- Guinea pigs are more sociable than hamsters.
- Guinea pigs live longer than hamsters.
- Some guinea pigs require a lot of grooming.
- A hamster cage won't take up as much room as a guinea pig **pen**.

ABYSSINIAN GUINEA PIG

This cute guinea pig is popular because of its fabulous hairstyle. Its fur grows in spiky swirls called rosettes that create its distinct look. The Abyssinian needs to be **groomed** often and it can be quite mischievous.

2 years **6 years**

Hamsters live an average of two years while guinea pigs live an average of six years.

SYRIAN HAMSTER

If you've ever been to a pet store, you've probably spotted this little guy. Syrian hamsters are often golden brown in color and grow to around 6 inches (15 cm) long. Although they like spending time with their owners, they don't like sharing their cage with other hamsters.

CAMPBELL'S DWARF HAMSTER

These little fluffballs are about 4 inches (10 cm) long and silvery-gray in color. Campbell's **dwarf** hamsters are sociable and happy to share their cage with another hamster. They can be a bit more nervous than Syrian hamsters, so they don't like to be handled as much.

DID YOU KNOW?

Your guinea pig might jump around or do little hops when it is happy. This is called popcorning!

RARE RODENTS

From wild islanders to pets that need sunscreen, hamsters and guinea pigs have been living with humans for a long time.

SKINNY PIG

Skinny pigs don't look like your average guinea pigs! They are born without hair, so they need to eat a bit more food to keep their body temperature up. But in most other ways they are just like other guinea pigs and have calm, sociable personalities.

DID YOU KNOW?

Skinny pigs have similar skin to humans, so if you take them outdoors they need to wear sunscreen to keep their skin from burning!

DWARF WINTER WHITE RUSSIAN HAMSTER

Dwarf hamsters are a common type of pet hamster, but it is quite rare to find a dwarf winter white Russian hamster. These hamsters have pure-white fur, and most have gray patches on their noses and ears.

EUROPEAN HAMSTER

This wild **species** of hamster can grow up to 14 inches (35 cm) long and has distinct black fur on its belly. The European hamster has become endangered in some areas because it is hunted for its fur or because farmers see it as a pest. However, scientists are working to protect this species.

SANTA CATARINA'S GUINEA PIG

This rare guinea pig comes from a tiny island in the state of Santa Catarina, Brazil. There are only 45 to 60 of these rodents left in the world, which makes them a **critically endangered** species.

PERSONALITY TRAITS

With tiny paws and twitchy noses, hamsters and guinea pigs are the sweetest pets around. Keep reading to discover how these furry companions are different, but the same in some ways too!

HAMSTERS

Most hamsters prefer to be kept alone in their cages. Keeping some types of hamsters in pairs could cause them to fight.

Hamsters are active at night and often keep their owners awake when they scurry around their cages.

Hamsters are very quiet when they squeak. In fact, some of their noises can only be heard by other hamsters!

SHHH...

GUINEA PIGS

Guinea pigs take short naps and are active both day and night.

HELLO THERE!

These clever pets can make about 11 unique sounds. When they get to know their owners, they start to chatter to them.

Guinea pigs can get lonely, so it is best to keep them in pairs (or more if you have the space).

TRAITS THEY SHARE

NIBBLING
They both love to **gnaw** and nibble on everything from cardboard to the sides of their cages.

PETTING
Guinea pigs and hamsters like to be petted, but hamsters might get fidgety and want to be put down.

RUNNING
They are both really active and love to run around, play with toys, and stretch their little legs.

PUPS

There are many differences between hamster and guinea pig babies—called pups—but they are both so cute!

HAMSTER PUPS

Hamsters are born blind, deaf, and completely furless, although it doesn't take them long to develop. After two weeks, they have fur and start to open their eyes. Hamster pups need to stay with their mothers until they are a month old. They should not be handled by humans before then.

Hamster babies soon start to look like miniature versions of their parents!

GUINEA PIG PUPS

Unlike hamsters, guinea pigs are born fully alert and with fur. In fact, they are just like tiny versions of full-grown guinea pigs! Guinea pig pups can be handled almost right away, so they get used to being around people very quickly.

Guinea pig pups don't waste any time. They want to begin exploring right away!

FACT FILE

■ Guinea pigs can eat some solid food right away, and grass after a few weeks.

■ A guinea pig pup weighs about the same as a bar of soap.

■ Most guinea pigs are about one month old when people take them home.

4 pups

20 pups

Guinea pigs have between two and four pups in a litter. Litters of hamsters can have up to 20 pups!

LITTLE PET, BIG LOVE!

Guinea pigs and hamsters are very easygoing pets, but these intelligent little animals still need a lot of love and attention to keep them happy.

DINNERTIME

Guinea pigs need to eat fresh fruit and vegetables, hay, and pellets that contain plenty of vitamins and minerals. They also need a bottle filled with fresh water attached to their cage or pen.

Hamsters should be given dry food containing the vitamins and minerals they need, as well as fresh fruit and vegetables such as carrots, bananas, and corn. They also need a bottle or bowl of fresh water in their cage.

KEEPING CLEAN

Guinea pigs like to keep clean and will do most of the cleaning themselves. They need to be brushed regularly and their nails should be trimmed once a month.

Hamsters like to keep themselves clean and tidy, and don't normally need to be washed or brushed.

DID YOU KNOW?

Not all lettuce is good for guinea pigs. Iceberg lettuce can give them bad stomach pains and cause health problems. Romaine lettuce is the best choice for these rodents.

FUN TIMES

Hamsters love to be entertained, so take your pet out of its cage at least once a day. Some hamsters like balls and wheels, but exploring and hiding are their favorite things to do. Try making a fun hamster tunnel using cardboard tubes.

Always keep an eye on your hamster when it is playing outside its cage!

Guinea pigs love to be social, which is why they should be kept with at least one other guinea pig—or even two or three! They also love to play and explore, so make sure you give them plenty of attention and freedom in a safe, secure area.

13

RODENT RULES

Can guinea pigs share a cage with other animals? What happens when hamsters eat too much? Avoid common mistakes by following these simple hints and tips.

HAMSTERS – DO:

✔

Get the right size wheel for your hamster. If the wheel is too big or too small, it could injure your pet's back.

✔

Scoop your hamster from underneath when you pick it up. If you grab the hamster from above, it might think you are a predator.

✔

Keep your eyes on your hamster when it is roaming free. These animals are small and can disappear very easily!

GUINEA PIGS – DO:

✔

Keep guinea pigs indoors when it is cold or very hot outside. They can easily get too cold or overheat.

✔

Research the right type of bedding to use in your pet's cage.
(Turn to page 17 to find out more.)

✔

Interact with your pet each day. Even if you don't have time to sit and play, make sure you say hello and give it some attention.

HAMSTERS - DON'T:

X

Don't wake up your hamster to play when it is sleeping. Hamsters usually like to sleep during the day.

X

Don't use a hamster wheel made of wire because it will damage your pet's feet.

X

Don't let your hamster eat too much food. Hamsters can become overweight and that causes health problems.

GUINEA PIGS - DON'T:

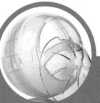

X

Don't put a guinea pig into a hamster ball. Unlike hamsters, guinea pigs have rigid backs that could get hurt inside the balls.

X

Don't use pine or cedar wood chips for bedding because they can be poisonous to small animals.

X

Don't keep guinea pigs in a cage with other animals, such as rabbits or ferrets. They won't get along and the guinea pigs could get hurt.

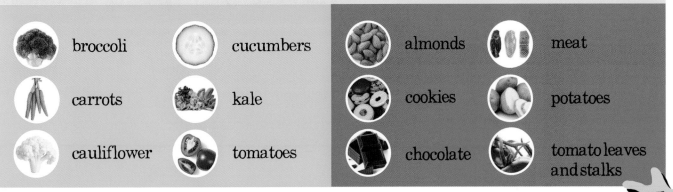

FOOD FOR HAMSTERS & GUINEA PIGS

✔

X

broccoli

cucumbers

carrots

kale

cauliflower

tomatoes

almonds

meat

cookies

potatoes

chocolate

tomato leaves and stalks

THE COZIEST CAGE

From choosing the right bedding to keeping your pet's cage clean, creating an interesting and cozy home for your furry little friend will keep it happy and healthy.

HAMSTER HOME

Your hamster's cage will need to be at least 31 inches (80 cm) by 20 inches (50 cm) and made of plastic, metal, or glass. If you choose a cage with metal bars, make sure they are close together to stop your hamster from escaping. Safely close the cage door after you have put your hamster back inside the cage.

BLISSFUL BEDDING

The floor of your pet's cage should have a thick layer of special hamster bedding. Never use sawdust or wood shavings because they could hurt your pet. You'll also need to put some nesting material in your hamster's **hidey house** —ripped up pieces of toilet paper work really well for this.

HOUSEWORK!

Bedding that has been **soiled** will need to be changed each day, and all bedding should be replaced once a week. Each month you should remove all bedding and toys and give your hamster's cage a good cleaning.

GUINEA PIG HOME

The more guinea pigs you have, the more space they will need. For two guinea pigs, the cage or pen will need to be at least 59 inches (150 cm) by 28 inches (70 cm). It's up to you whether you choose a pen or cage—both will keep your pet healthy and happy.

BEDTIME!

Guinea pig bedding can be made of paper, straw, or special guinea pig bedding material. You can make your pet's bedding extra soft by putting fleece blankets on the bottom of the cage before you start to add the bedding material.

GUINEA PIG HIDEWAY

Guinea pigs like to be entertained, but they also like to have dark places to snuggle up and hide. Wooden bridges, large tunnels, and soft hidey houses are perfect for playful guinea pigs.

DID YOU KNOW?

You can use bowls to feed hamsters and guinea pigs or scatter their food around their cages or a combination of both!

SCURRY THROUGH TIME

Discover the unusual history of the hamster and how guinea pigs were given as special gifts!

HAMSTER HISTORY

ALL BUT GONE
By the 1920s, Syrian hamsters had been hunted so much that they were nearly **extinct** and only a few of these rodents remained.

1700–1800	1920s	1930s

FIRST HAMSTERS
The first hamsters came from Syria. At one time, there were so many hamsters in the wild in Syria that farmers hunted them as pests and sold their fur.

AN AMAZING DISCOVERY
A scientist working in Syria discovered a female hamster and her babies. He **transported** them back to his home and bred them as pets to be sent around the world.

GUINEA PIG HISTORY

GUINEA PIG POWERS

■ In Peru around 2000 B.C.E., people used guinea pigs to detect evil spirits.

■ When the guinea pigs squeaked, people believed they had detected spirits.

■ Black guinea pigs were very rare and were seen as especially holy.

GUINEA PIG GIFTS

Around 1000 B.C.E., guinea pigs were often given as birthday gifts and even as wedding presents!

2000 B.C.E.	1000 B.C.E.	1700s

GUINEA PIG PROGRESS

Guinea pigs have been kept as pets for more than 4,000 years! They are native to South America and were kept for food and as pets for children in Peru and Bolivia.

ON THE MOVE

When traders from Europe came to South America, they took guinea pigs back with them and the rodents became popular pets around the world.

FAMOUS FURBALLS

From the White House to Hollywood movies, hamsters and guinea pigs are just too cute not to be famous!

HAMSTER HEROES

RHINO

In 2008, the world was introduced to a hamster named Rhino in *Bolt*, a movie about a TV dog who thinks he has superpowers. Rhino is Bolt's biggest fan, and although he spends most of his time in an exercise ball, the hamster became so popular that Disney made a short film all about him!

SOCCER SUPERSTAR

When you think sports team mascot, you might think brave lion or even dancing bull. But hefty hamster? That's right! Hammy the Hamster is the mascot of Scottish soccer team Hamilton Academical F.C. Fans of the team love watching Hammy warm up the crowd before each home game.

GUINEA PIG STARS

PRESIDENTIAL PETS

Theodore Roosevelt (1858–1919) was the 26th president of the United States—and a big fan of guinea pigs! His pets became the most famous guinea pigs in the 1900s and had names like Admiral Dewey, Dr. Johnson, Bob Evans, Bishop Doan, and Father O'Grady.

DID YOU KNOW?

Queen Elizabeth I (1533–1603) had a pet guinea pig.

NORMAN

A 2016 movie called *The Secret Life of Pets* tells the story of two apartment dogs that struggle to survive in New York. But it also introduces us to many other pets in the city—including Norman, a happy guinea pig who's always up for adventure!

RODENT RECORDS

From long-lived hamsters to speedy guinea pigs, take a look at the world's most remarkable rodents.

58 species

3 species

There are 58 species of rodents on the list of critically endangered animals, three of which may be extinct.

QUICK AS A FLASH!

In 2009, a guinea pig named Flash was recorded running 33 feet (10 m) in just 8.81 seconds.

HAMSTER'S GIANT COUSIN!

The capybara is sometimes described as the world's biggest hamster, but it's actually not a hamster at all. It is the world's largest rodent, though, and can grow up to 25 inches (64 cm) tall and more than 3.3 feet (1 m) long!

Пятипалый карликовый тушканчик
ПОЧТА СССР
3ᴷ
1985

This stamp was used in the former Soviet Union more than 30 years ago to celebrate the jerboa.

DID YOU KNOW?

The oldest hamster lived for four and a half years.

TEENY-TINY RELATIONS

The Baluchistan pygmy jerboa is the smallest rodent on Earth—and possibly the cutest! It measures only 1.6 inches (4 cm) tall. It stands and hops on its hind legs, which makes it look more like a tiny kangaroo than a rodent.

ALL ABOUT RODENTS

- There are more than 2,000 species of rodents in the world.
- They include everything from squirrels to porcupines.
- Rodents' teeth never stop growing, which is why these animals like to nibble and gnaw.

THE LONG-ISH JUMP

Truffles holds the record for the longest jump by a guinea pig. In 2012, he managed to leap over a gap measuring 18.9 inches (48 cm), which is quite a stunt for a pet with such little legs!

0 inches   18.9 inches

DID YOU KNOW?

The oldest guinea pig lived for 15 years.

FIVE FACTS

Would you like to know even more about your favorite rodent pets? Keep reading to discover more fabulous facts!

1 VERY CHEEKY!

Hamsters store food in their cheeks to eat later. The food can make their bulging cheeks double in size!

2 TOE TO TOE

Guinea pigs have four toes on their front paws and only three toes on their back paws.

3 HAMSTERS ON THE MOVE

Hamsters are crepuscular, which means they are most actve in the early morning and early evening.

4 WHAT'S IN A NAME?

Guinea pigs are not pigs and they do not come from the country Guinea in Africa. It is believed they got their piggy name because of the high-pitched squeaks they make.

5 RODENTS IN A ROW

When guinea pigs walk together, they always line up in single file with the largest guinea pig at the front and the pup in the middle.

YOUR FAVORITE FURRY FRIEND

Can you match your personality to your dream pet?
Answer the questions and follow the arrows to find out!

Cute!

Relaxing

DO YOU PREFER BEING WITH FRIENDS OR RELAXING ON YOUR OWN?

WHAT'S BETTER: SMALL AND CUTE OR FURRY AND FRIENDLY?

Friendly!

Afternoon

Being with friends

ARE YOU A MORNING PERSON OR AN AFTERNOON PERSON?

Morning

Not sure

Maybe

DOES YOUR HOME HAVE PLENTY OF ROOM?

WOULD YOU LIKE MORE THAN ONE TYPE OF PET?

Yes!

Yes!

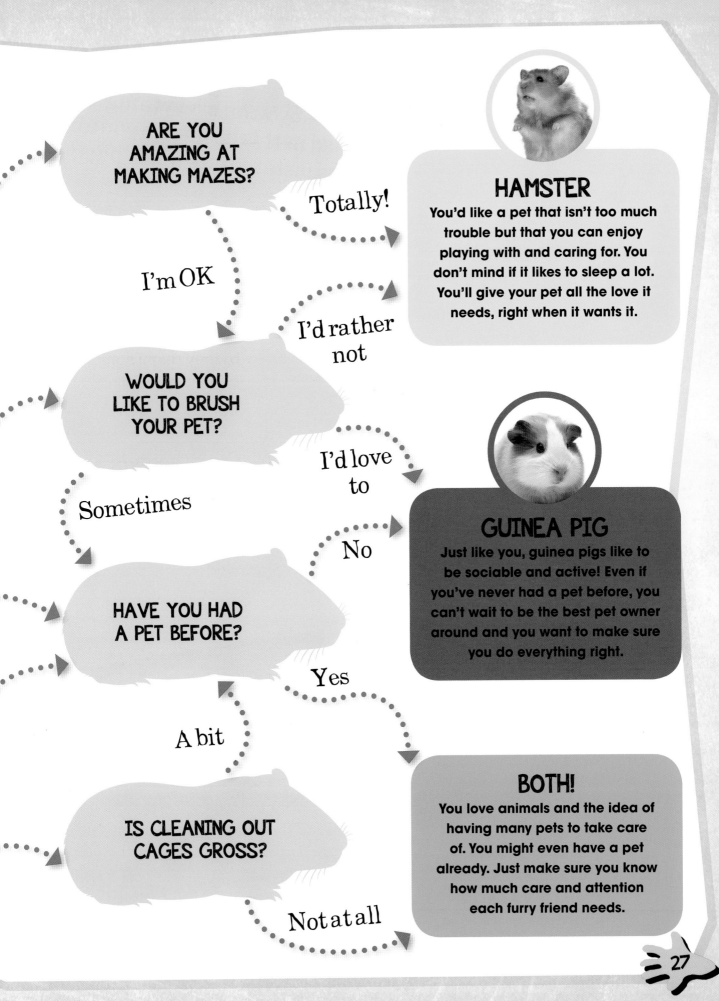

ARE YOU AMAZING AT MAKING MAZES?

Totally!

I'm OK

I'd rather not

WOULD YOU LIKE TO BRUSH YOUR PET?

Sometimes

I'd love to

No

HAVE YOU HAD A PET BEFORE?

A bit

Yes

IS CLEANING OUT CAGES GROSS?

Not at all

HAMSTER

You'd like a pet that isn't too much trouble but that you can enjoy playing with and caring for. You don't mind if it likes to sleep a lot. You'll give your pet all the love it needs, right when it wants it.

GUINEA PIG

Just like you, guinea pigs like to be sociable and active! Even if you've never had a pet before, you can't wait to be the best pet owner around and you want to make sure you do everything right.

BOTH!

You love animals and the idea of having many pets to take care of. You might even have a pet already. Just make sure you know how much care and attention each furry friend needs.

QUIZ!

It's time to test you on everything you have learned in this book! Are you an expert on hamsters and guinea pigs?

1 WHAT IS IT CALLED WHEN GUINEA PIGS DO LITTLE JUMPS AND HOPS?

a) pop dancing
b) pop hopping
c) popcorning

2 WHAT IS THE NAME OF THE HAIRLESS BREED OF GUINEA PIG?

a) skinny pig
b) bald pig
c) furless pig

3 WHY CAN'T MOST HAMSTERS BE KEPT IN PAIRS?

a) they could spread diseases
b) they might fight
c) they stop eating

4 WHICH RODENTS ARE BORN BLIND?

a) hamsters
b) guinea pigs
c) both

The answers can be found on page 30.

5 WHICH RODENTS WOULD LOVE EXERCISE WHEELS IN THEIR CAGES?

a) hamsters
b) guinea pigs
c) both

6 WHY SHOULDN'T YOU KEEP GUINEA PIGS WITH OTHER SPECIES OF PETS?

a) they might get hurt
b) they'll steal all the food
c) they'll hide all the time

7 HOW OFTEN SHOULD YOU GIVE YOUR HAMSTER'S CAGE A THOROUGH CLEANING?

a) once a year
b) once a week
c) once a month

8 WHICH ENGLISH QUEEN HAD
A GUINEA PIG AS A PET?

a) Queen Mary
b) Queen Elizabeth I
c) Queen Victoria

9 WHAT WAS THE NAME
OF THE HAMSTER IN
THE DISNEY MOVIE
BOLT?

a) Rhino
b) Hippo
c) Wolf

10 WHAT IS THE
LARGEST RODENT
IN THE WORLD?

a) the hare
b) the capybara
c) the porcupine

GLOSSARY

bedding
The material used to line your pet's home and make a bed

breed
A group of animals with similar characteristics and appearances

coat
An animal's fur

critically endangered
Describing animals at high risk of dying out in the wild

dwarf
Smaller than average size

extinct
Describing an animal or plant that no longer exists

gnaw
To keep biting and nibbling

groom
To brush and clean your pet

hidey house
An enclosed, dark area for your pet to snuggle up in

holy
Connected to a god or a religion

litter
A group of baby animals born at the same time to the same mother

pen
A fence-like enclosure for animals

predator
An animal that hunts other animals for food

rodent
One of a group of animals that includes hamsters, guinea pigs, rats, and mice

sociable
Liking to be around others

soiled
Covered in pee or poop

species
A group of similar living things that can reproduce

transport
To move something from one place to another

INDEX